The Stoic And The Epicurean

Systems Of Morals

Woodbridge Riley

Kessinger Publishing's Rare Reprints

Thousands of Scarce and Hard-to-Find Books on These and other Subjects!

- Americana
- Ancient Mysteries
- Animals
- Anthropology
- Architecture
- Arts
- Astrology
- Bibliographies
- Biographies & Memoirs
- Body, Mind & Spirit
- Business & Investing
- Children & Young Adult
- Collectibles
- Comparative Religions
- Crafts & Hobbies
- Earth Sciences
- Education
- Ephemera
- Fiction
- Folklore
- Geography
- Health & Diet
- History
- Hobbies & Leisure
- Humor
- Illustrated Books
- Language & Culture
- Law
- Life Sciences

- Literature
- Medicine & Pharmacy
- Metaphysical
- Music
- Mystery & Crime
- Mythology
- Natural History
- Outdoor & Nature
- Philosophy
- Poetry
- Political Science
- Science
- Psychiatry & Psychology
- Reference
- Religion & Spiritualism
- Rhetoric
- Sacred Books
- Science Fiction
- Science & Technology
- Self-Help
- Social Sciences
- Symbolism
- Theatre & Drama
- Theology
- Travel & Explorations
- War & Military
- Women
- Yoga
- *Plus Much More!*

We kindly invite you to view our catalog list at:
http://www.kessinger.net

PART FOUR

STOICS AND EPICUREANS

I. STOICISM

"GREEK philosophy, like Greek art, is the offspring of Greek political independence. In the whirl of public life everyone is thrown on himself and his own resources. Thereby, and by the emulation begotten of unlimited competition for all the good things of life, the Greek had learned to make full use of his intellect. Consciousness of his dignity—which a Greek associated far more closely than we do with the privilege of citizenship—and independence of the necessity of struggling for daily food, had taught him independence of mind, and enabled him to devote himself to the pursuit of knowledge without any ulterior aim. With the decline of political independence the mental powers of the nation were broken past remedy. No longer borne up by a powerful *esprit de corps*, weaned from the habit of working for the common weal, the majority gave themselves up to the petty interests of private life and personal affairs. Even the better disposed were too much occupied in contending against the low tone and corruption of their times to be able to devote themselves in moments of relaxation to independent speculation. What could be expected in such an age as that which preceded the rise of the Stoic and Epicurean systems, but that philosophy would become practical itself, if indeed it were studied at all?

"An age like that did not require theoretical knowledge, but it did require moral bracing and strengthening. If these were not to be had from popular religion in its then state, was it matter for wonder that philosophy should be looked to to supply the deficiency, seeing that in all cultivated circles philosophy had already taken the place of religion? If we ask in what form, and in what form only, philosophy could supply the deficiency under the then circumstances, the answer is not far to seek. There was little room for creative effort, plenty for sustained endurance; little for activity without, plenty for activity within; little room for public life, plenty of room for private life. So utterly hopeless had the public state of Greece become that even the few who made it their business to provide a remedy could only gain for themselves the honour of martyrdom. As matters stood, the only course open for the best-intentioned was to withdraw entirely within themselves, to entrench themselves within the safe barriers of their inner life against outward misfortunes, and to make happiness dependent entirely on their own inward state.

"Stoic apathy, Epicurean self-contentment, and Sceptic imperturbability were the doctrines which suited the political helplessness of the age, and they were therefore the doctrines which met with the most general acceptance. There was yet another which suited it—viz., the sinking of national distinctions in the feeling of a common humanity, the severance of morals from politics which characterises the philosophy of the Alexandrian and Roman periods. The barriers which kept nations apart had been swept away, together with their national independence: East and West, Greeks and barbarians, were united in large empires, brought into communicatioh and forced into comparison with one another in matters the most important. Philosophy declared that all men are of one blood and are equally privileged citizens of one empire, that morality rests on the relation of man to man, and is independent of nationality and position in the state; but in so doing it only explicitly stated a truth which was partly realized and partly implied in actual life."—ZELLER: *Stoics, Epicureans, and Sceptics.*

THE SCHOOL OF DISCIPLINE

To Aristotle the highest happiness is found in the vision of truth, in the pursuit of wisdom as such. In this he connects himself both with his predecessors and his successors. The old Pythagorean brotherhood had a similar aim, so had the Platonic Academy, and now Aristotle's own school, the Peripatetic, under Theophrastus, sought to carry the quest forward. But the scene changes. With the overlordship of Macedonia and Rome, Greece lost its liberty. The Athenians were no longer free men who could vary their political activities with philosophic speculations. Hence the philosophic schools changed their character and became a mental refuge, just as did the colleges in the South after the Civil War when the soldier often became the scholar. The analogy is curiously close when we read that after the conquest of Alexander thoughtful and original men sought in scientific ethics an occupation for the loss of public life, and consolation for the misconstruction put upon their retirement by noisy patriots.[1]

Such a mental refuge was the Stoa, that public porch or colonnade of Athens which gave the school its name. Here another change

---

J. P. Mahaffy, *Greek Life and Thought*, p. 4.

took place. Serious men might turn to philosophy, but philosophy itself was turned to ethics rather than metaphysics, to practical happiness rather than to speculation as an end in itself. In many cases the results were remarkable. The Stoics were valued both privately and publicly. They were sometimes called in professionally to minister to those in sorrow; at other times to negotiate with foreign powers as when a trio of representative philosophers were sent to Rome to obtain better terms from the conqueror.

In general the Stoic was a creature of practical morality and came to be a familiar figure throughout the Roman Empire, known outwardly by his cloak and staff, inwardly by his insistency on the majesty of duty, the splendour of devotion, the dignity of self-denial. To understand what this ancient travelling thinker meant to the public, we may compare him to Emerson, who was welcome by the men and women of the far frontier who had a hard row to hoe and were braced by the Sage of Concord, preaching his doctrines of courage and self-reliance. The Stoics were the best known of the later Greek moralists; in fact, their influence was so strong as to justify the ancient paradox that captive Greece led Rome itself into captivity. In the terrible times of the civil wars and the nightmare reign of Nero the Stoics were especially effective. They consoled those who needed the consolation of philosophy, teaching that the accidents and misfortunes of life are nothing to him who has a serene belief in providence.

This is Stoicism in its simplicity. Its rise and development, however, were complicated. The school had its rivals. There were the Cynics, who took their name from their doglike manners, as when Diogenes growled from his tub that the only favour he wanted from the great Alexander was that the latter should keep out of his light. There were the Epicureans, who sought a state of undisturbedness, and were so opposed to the strenuous life that they held that happiness consisted in the avoidance of all excitements and disturbances. The garden of Epicurus, with its freedom from perturbations, was for many a place of perpetual vacation, far from the madding crowd, a place where it was bad form to discuss public questions, and where disagreeably earnest people were not wanted. This, at least, was the school as it was portrayed by its critics. But Epicurus himself was no sterile dilettante and his doctrine was not one of mere self-indulgence. Still, many an Epicurean looked forward to the "garden" as a means of escape from the cares and troubles of this world, just as a weary man of affairs dreams of ending his days on the Riviera.

But to return to the Stoic. Those who prefer the Epicurean land of the lotus-eater have portrayed him as a dismal Johnny, a mere kill-joy belonging to that species of social reformer and uplifter for whose suppression the easy-going citizen often longs. Such a portrayal is an exaggeration. The Stoic had much sense and moderation and was above all practical. Zeno, the founder, arrived in Athens as a stranger from Cyprus and, according to the story, first came into contact with Crates the Cynic. From the latter and his followers he learned the principle of self-sufficiency, but did not follow them in their churlish disregard for the social amenities. As the saying is, he accepted Diogenes without the tub. The Cynic was wont to withdraw into his shell, to avoid public affairs, and to disdain the current beliefs in patriotism and religion. But the Stoic, though meditative, did not identify the inner life with isolation; he advised his disciples to mix in affairs, to attain the larger patriotism of the citizen of the world, and to see that in all religions there was a common element, the providential care of the gods for men.

Cynicism was one thing, civilization another. Overwhelmed with the complexities of society, the Cynic took the easy rôle of over-simplification—disregard for dress, contempt for society, and a general attitude that whatever is is wrong. They called this the state of nature and actually taught that animals and savages were better off than man. According to the accounts, Diogenes in his personal habits was as shameless as a dog, while Antisthenes, the founder of the school, held that primitive man was a law unto himself.

There was little of this in the Stoics. They were not anti-social; they did not confuse a return to nature with a return to bestiality, nor did they follow the other extreme of Aristotle, who taught that man's highest aim is a life of leisure, spent in meditation, "thinking upon thought." The Stoic rôle was different; it was to be a man among men, whether in the common round, the daily task, or in the vexatious affairs of statecraft. Here, then, we find a wide range of representatives, from Epictetus, the slave, to Marcus Aurelius Antoninus, the emperor, the one standing for Stoicism in the cottage, the other for Stoicism on the throne.

The system was a livable system. In its second or Roman period it has come down to us not only in Epictetus's *Handbook*, and in Marcus Aurelius's *Meditations Addressed to Himself*, but in Cicero's work entitled *On Duties*, and Seneca's entitled *Of a Happy Life*. These works left their mark on the civilized world and many traces of them are to be found here and there. Thus Epictetus was recommended for the use of students by Thomas Jefferson and reprinted in his day in the original Greek at Philadelphia. The writings of

Marcus Aurelius and Seneca are still to be had in popular editions, while Tully's *Offices*, as Cicero's *De Officiis* was called, was often referred to by the Southern gentlemen of the old school.

This is part of the external history of the documents. The inner doctrines are the following: a belief in the goodness of the gods, in the moral government of the world, and in providence, and along with these a facing of the problem of evil and a final attitude of resignation and acquiescence in the course of events. The belief in the goodness of the gods was based on the conception of the world as a cosmos or orderly universe. Here the forerunners of Socrates were utilized by the earliest Stoics. They went as far back as Heraclitus, who taught that "this one order of things was created by none of the gods, nor yet by any of mankind, but it ever was, and is, and shall be, eternal fire—ignited by measure, and extinguished by measure." This order, in turn, is guaranteed by Logos, reason, which is everlasting although "men are unable to comprehend it before they have heard it or even after they have heard it for the first time." This primordial fire is divine and eternal, hence Zeno argues that man partakes of it, since human reason is a spark of the celestial flame. This doctrine, naturally, led to further inferences. The divine fire being the primitive substance from which all things derive, then those that possess it, especially man in his rational soul, are privileged by nature to hold communion with God. And so, concludes Marcus Aurelius, being united to Him in intercourse through reason, why may not a man then call himself a citizen of the world, why not a son of God?

The origins and inferences of Stoicism are consistent. But Zeno, the founder, drew from still other sources than Heraclitus. Socrates had discoursed at length on the wisdom and goodness of the gods toward the sons of men, while Plato, in his prose poem of creation, had put these words into the mouth of the imaginary philosopher Timæus: "We shall do well in believing on the testimony of wise men. God desired that all things should be good and nothing bad, so far as this was attainable." So, too, Aristotle, in opposing the anarchic atomists, believers in blind chance, had argued for an intelligent adaption of means to ends in the creation.

All this meant a purposive government of the world and such purposiveness was none other than providence. We Stoics, as you know, says Seneca, distinguish in nature cause and matter as conditions for all becoming. Matter is inert, indifferent to all determinations, and will remain in a state of rest unless it be moved. Cause or reason shapes matter and turns it at will in any direction, producing out of matter a variety of objects. In other words, that out of which all things are made must be distinct from that by which all things are made and this is what is meant by matter and cause. These are the positive points and are summed up in that single fragment of early Stoic doctrine that has come down to us unimpaired. This is the famous "Hymn to Zeus" by Cleänthes:

> O God most glorious, called by many a name,
> Nature's great King, through endless years the same;
> Omnipotence, who by thy just decree
> Controllest all, hail, Zeus, for unto thee
> Behoves thy creatures in all lands to call.
> We are thy children, we alone, of all
> On earth's broad ways that wander to and fro,
> Bearing thine image wheresoe'er we go.
> Wherefore with songs of praise thy power I will forth show.
> Lo! yonder heaven, that round the earth is wheeled,
> Follows thy guidance, still to thee doth yield
> Glad homage; thine unconquerable hand
> Such flaming minister, the levin-brand,
> Wieldeth, a sword two-edged, whose deathless might
> Pulsates through all that Nature brings to light;
> Vehicle of the universal Word, that flows
> Through all, and in the light celestial glows
> Of stars both great and small. O King of Kings
> Through ceaseless ages, God, whose purpose brings
> To birth whate'er on land or in the sea
> Is wrought, or in high heaven's immensity;
> Save what the sinner works infatuate.
> Nay, but thou knowest to make crooked straight:
> Chaos to thee is order: in thine eyes
> The unloved is lovely, who did'st harmonise
> Things evil with things good, that there should be
> One Word through all things everlastingly.
> One Word—whose voice alas! the wicked spurn;
> Insatiate for the good their spirits yearn:
> Yet seeing see not, neither hearing hear
> God's universal law, which those revere,
> By reason guided, happiness who win.
> The rest, unreasoning, diverse shapes of sin
> Self-prompted follow: for an idle name
> Vainly they wrestle in the lists of fame:
> Others inordinately Riches woo,
> Or dissolute, the joys of flesh pursue.
> Now here, now there they wander, fruitless still,
> For ever seeking good and finding ill.
> Zeus the all-bountiful, whom darkness shrouds,
> Whose lightning lightens in the thunder clouds;
> Thy children save from error's deadly sway:
> Turn thou the darkness from their souls away:

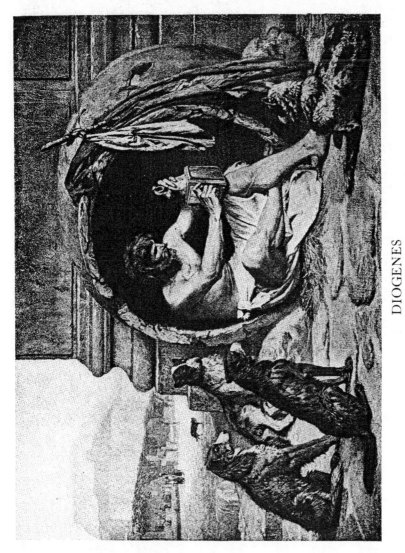

DIOGENES

In his tub—lighting his lantern to search out an honest man

Vouchsafe that unto knowledge they attain;
For thou by knowledge art made strong to reign
O'er all, and all things rulest righteously.
So by thee honoured, we will honour thee,
Praising thy works continually with songs,
As mortals should; nor higher meed belongs
E'en to the gods, than justly to adore
The universal law for evermore.

THE GUIDE OF LIFE

"A brave man must expect to be taught, for he is to steer his course in the teeth of fortune, and to work against wind and weather. In the sufferings of torments, though there appear but one virtue, a man exercises many. That which is most eminent is patience (which is but a branch of fortitude); but there is prudence also in the choice of the action and in the bearing what we cannot avoid, and there is constancy in bearing it resolutely; and there is the same concurrence also of several virtues in other generous undertakings. When Leonidas was to carry his three hundred men into the straits of Thermopylæ, to put a stop to Xerxes's huge army—'Come, fellow-soldiers,' says he, 'eat your dinners here as if you were to sup in another world'; and they answered his resolution. How plain and imperious was that short speech of Calditius to his men upon a desperate action, and how glorious a mixture was there in it both of bravery and prudence! 'Soldiers,' says he, 'it is necessary for us to go, but it is not necessary for us to return.'"—*The Morals of Seneca*, Chapter XVI.

With their doctrines of the goodness of God and the moral government of the world and providence the Stoics sought a practical system. Their aim was to make men, and their motto, adopted by a later learned society, was: "Philosophy the Guide of Life." Already two rival schools had sought to solve the problem but this was in a negative way, by withdrawal from life. Thus Diogenes in disgust had rejected the very things which Greek civilization had gained, having little use for art, letters, and science. His was a kind of paradoxical bravery in trying to live like an animal without house or home, pleasures or possessions. Epicurus, in contrast, had lent himself to a certain cowardice; as the slave Epictetus later said: he disowned all manly offices, those of a father of a family, of a citizen, and of a friend.

Stoicism was opposed to both these attitudes. It sought not

only to guide the private life of the individual and the common life of the state, but to furnish consolation in times of trouble and distress. One great means toward this is for man to realize that he is part and parcel of the universe, that as such he partakes of its law and order. Here the Stoics compared life to a drama in which God has given each man his lines to learn, his part to play, whatever be the outcome. In this world he is not a mere puppet, a marionette pulled by the strings of an unseen fate. He is rather one who coöperates with the divine providence, for to him the world is rational and he, as portion of the world, partakes of its rationality. Zeno, the founder, called this living in conformity to nature. By this he meant not a return to the ways of the beasts but rather to "the ways of the stars." The thing sounds poetic; it was meant to be scientific. The age of Zeno was an age of new discoveries in astronomy, and of the formation of that system of regularly revolving orbs which led to the inference that order is heaven's first law. We men, then, as parts of the universal system, belong to a law-and-order league; as partakers of the divine fire we are of like nature with Zeus, the guide and governor of the universe. In this we are not blind instruments of a blind fate, but conscious agents coöperating with that "seeing force which runs things."

If there is order there is purpose, so reasoned the Stoics, and though this purpose may often be inscrutable to us, it nevertheless exists. As "God always geometrizes," though we may not know the final solution of the problem, so the divine playwright has a plot to be logically unfolded. The world's a stage in which we await our exits and our entrances. In these actions, of course, we may often miss our cues, but in whatever parts we have been cast we should do our best, just as those supernumeraries, the lower creatures, fulfil their proper functions. Nature is an unfolding process where the different orders have their destiny: the acorn grows into the oak, the foolish puppy into a faithful hound, the playing child into the earnest man. Nature then means orderly growth; the man with a natural capacity for virtue can fulfil his function in whatever state in his life it has pleased God to place him, whether as a slave or as an emperor.

This scheme is noble; at the same time there is in it a call to resignation. This is to be met by an appeal to reason and an appeal to duty. Thus Epictetus the slave says: "For this purpose God leads me hither and thither, shows me to men as poor, without authority, and sick, not because he does not care for me, but with a view of exercising me and of using me as a witness to others." So, too, Marcus Aurelius the emperor, speaking to himself of death, says:

"The day that you dread as though it were your last is the birthday of eternity." In this sublime utterance there is the implication that this life with its duties is a preparation for another life with even greater responsibilities. We start with certain disabilities such as leanings to ease and pleasure, but we are "God's athletes" and must undergo strict training, or, in even severer terms, we must be drastically cured of our moral ailings: "The philosopher's school, ye men, is a surgery; you ought not to go out of it pleased, but pained."

These are some of the more austere sayings of the Stoics called out by hard social or political conditions of a great slave or a great emperor. Such advices were utilized by a less commanding figure like Cicero, who as an eclectic found solace in Stoic doctrines. His *Tusculan Disputations* deal with the proper attitude in the face of sorrow, pain, and death. At one time he strives to comfort himself for the loss of his daughter, at another to brace himself at the threatened proscription of the Republican party. But in his treatise "On Duties" Cicero comes down to the level of ordinary affairs in which the Stoics were so effective. Such are the outward proprieties of speech and conversation, of domestic arrangements, of tact and behaviour, of honourable and dishonourable modes of life.

Another eclectic who utilized and applied the moral science of the Stoics was the historian Plutarch, who summarized the matter as follows: As exercise and medicine provide for the body's health and strength, so philosophy alone can cure the weakness or the sickness of the soul. By her help man learns to distinguish the noble from the base, the just from the unjust, the things worthy of our choice from those which we should shun; she teaches him how he ought to act in all the relations of his social life, warning him to fear the gods, honour his parents, respect old age, obey the laws, submit to governors, be loving to his friends, show self-control with womankind, tenderness with children, moderation with his slaves—above all, not to triumph overmuch in prosperous days, or to be cast down in adversity, not to be overmastered by pleasure, or brutalized by passion.

Stoicism was a livable system; it met the demands not only of the extremes in society, the slave or the emperor, but of the larger intermediate group of practical men of affairs. But this was the developed system after some of its difficulties had been smoothed down. These difficulties clustered about the baffling problem of evil. The founders of the school, in order to encourage themselves in times of trouble and adversity, had erected a great scheme of optimism.

Zeno began his lectures in the Stoa at Athens in the very year in which the city was besieged by the Macedonians and suffered from a consuming famine. In this there was an ironical contrast between the place where the philosopher taught and the conditions which he faced. While the Stoa was an artistic pantheon of war with its famous painting of the Greek victory at Marathon, the outlook for the city was anything but hopeful, for Athens itself now lay at the mercy of a military despot.

Furthermore, by this time the traditional religions of the Greek states had nearly collapsed. In the opinion of the wise, Homer had been "whipped out of the lists," and the old gods had gone. There was then a need to meet this double loss, political and religious. This need was met not only by the Stoic's confidence in his being a cosmopolite, a citizen of the world, but by his worship of nature. To him the cosmos, as an orderly universe, became the embodiment of reason, man being a part inherent in the greater whole. So to the Stoic, as a thoroughgoing pantheist, all were but parts of one stupendous whole, "whose body nature is and God the soul." This soul of the world may be variously called God, providence, destiny, fate, the seminal ether, and especially fire, the most subtle of all substances, which is diffused throughout matter as water through a sponge.

This is the first and greatest paradox. The Stoics were materialists, yet fervently religious; insistent on destiny and fate, yet ever appealing to man's free will, and all the time high optimists. To them the world, and all that therein is, is the product of divine power, is itself divine and therefore necessarily perfect. The Deity is active reason, manipulates matter and fashions all things to His end: "All that thou seest," says Lucan, "yea, all that moves, is God." This is the natural theology of the Stoics which was later accommodated to the popular mythology, since the universe, being God, the one supreme being, may be addressed as Zeus. Moreover, being divine in its totality, it is divine in its parts; hence the heavenly bodies may be worshipped as gods, also men of rare achievements are worshipful—heroes like Heracles and Odysseus; and, in the last stages of Stoicism, the very founders of the older school, Zeno, Cleanthes, and Chrysippus are worthy of worship. This deification of the Stoic sage, as the supremely wise man, approached perilously near to the later historic conceit—the worship of humanity. To a certain degree this was inevitable. To a man without a country, who had likewise lost his reverence for the gods of his people, there must be something to fill the void. So a system of morality embodied in the lives of men conspicuously good was a substitute for a lost land and a lost religion.

Under a despot like Demetrius, the spoiler of cities, or under a madman like Nero, it was proper to look on character as something fundamental, admirable, and worthy of worship. Man may become divine provided his ideal is divine. As Seneca puts the rule of life: So live among men, as if the eye of God were upon you; and so address yourself to God, as if men heard your prayer.

This is a high ideal, yet according to the Stoics it was not impossible of fulfilment. One significant line declares: "God is at home in the human body." This followed from a confidence in the will of God as revealed in the heart and conscience of those who seek to know that will. In other words, we are living in a cosmos, in a system of order, coherence, and reason, so in living according to nature we follow reason—and the end of reason is virtue. Man as a rational animal is therefore to carry on the work of the world. That which began as fire mist had implicit within it the divine reason. At the other end of the scale of being, in this later age of cosmic development, emerges man as a rational being, who must endeavour to steer a straight course. To rational man, then, philosophy becomes the art of living, just as navigation is the art of sailing.

THE ART OF LIVING

"For my part I think the old man should be sitting here, not to devise how ye may have no mean thoughts, nor speak no mean nor ignoble things about yourselves, but to watch that there arise not among us youths of such a mind, that when they have perceived their kinship with the Gods, and how the flesh and its possessions are laid upon us like bonds, and how many necessities for the management of life are by them brought upon us, they may desire to fling these things away for abhorred and intolerable burthens, and depart unto their kin. And this is what your master and teacher—if, in sooth, ye had any such—should have to contend with in you—that ye should come to him and say, 'Epictetus, we can endure no longer being bound to this body, giving it food and drink, and resting it and cleansing it, and going about to court one man after another for its sake. Are not such things indifferent and nothing to us? And is not death no evil? Are we not in some way kinsmen of God, and did we not come from Him? Let us depart to whence we came; let us be delivered at last from these bonds wherewith we are bound and burthened! Here are robbers, and thieves, and law courts, and those that are called tyrants, which through the body and its possessions seem as if they had some power over us. Let us show them that they have no power over any man!' And to this it should be my part to say, 'My friends, wait upon God. When He Himself shall give the signal and release you from this service, then are ye released unto Him. But for the present, bear to dwell in this place, wherein He has set you. Short, indeed, is this time of your sojourn, and easy to bear for those that are so minded. For what tyrant or what thief is there any longer, or what court'of law is terrible to one who thus makes nothing of the body and the possessions of it? Remain, then, and depart not without a reason.' Some such part as this should the teacher have to play toward the well-natured among his disciples."—*The Teachings of Epictetus*, Chapter IX.

The Stoics compared man to an apprentice who strives to imitate the master pilot, reason. But the waters of life are troubled and it is hard to steer a straight course. So like good navigators they sought guiding beacons and definite range lights. It was one thing to have a vague hope that all would come out well; it was another to know exactly what to seek and what to avoid. These, then, were their sailing directions: Follow the four cardinal virtues—prudence, manly courage, temperance, and justice; avoid the four primary passions—delight, desire, grief, and fear. Now while delight and desire have to do with good, and grief and fear with evil, yet it was the business of philosophy to avoid even things considered by many to be good. There were certain pleasures of eating and drinking which might seem harmless, but the Stoics' chief rivals, the Epicureans, in their search for pleasure had released a fatal formula when they spoke approvingly of the "sweetness of life." As the pursuit of pleasant things may lead to excess, it is better to stop our ears to them as did Odysseus to the Sirens. Much more did the Stoics steer clear of the opposites of delight and desire, namely grief and fear. These were denounced as furies which infest the life of fools; to give way to these emotions is the mark of a weakling; in grief there is selfish indulgence and in fear a sure sign that man has lost his presence of mind.

Curiously enough in these latter admonitions the Stoics had borrowed from their rivals. Epicurus himself had advised his followers not to give way to grief, not to torture themselves with unnecessary terrors; in short, to fear no evil either from gods or men. Here common conditions brought common advice; the refugee founder of Epicureanism, whose family was pursued by the Thracians, resembled the expatriate Stoics who advised undisturbedness even in physical torment. Thus Posidonius on his sick couch exclaimed: "You are making no impression, pain! Although you are hard to bear, I will never admit that you are an evil." Such advice came down the ages. It was this hard endurance that led the American colonists to call the silent Indian chief, tortured at the stake, a stoical savage. But the virtue of apathy, in turn, had its defects. It was what the poet called "virtue fix'd as in a front." At times it sounded downright cold-blooded. Apathy wiped out sympathy, as when the Stoic defined pity as "the vice of a petty spirit." The Roman senator Seneca, high in office, may have believed this, but the slave Epictetus corrected it. To him man was not to be emotionless like a statue. Those, too, were wrong who advised against marriage and the bringing up of children because of the anxiety such relations might entail. To such Epictetus declared that, while man should be a Stoic, a Stoic should be a man and should take up the duties of husband and citizen. This advice is directed against the extremists of the school, rigorous Stoics who laid themselves open to ridicule. With the latter apathy ranged from an indifference to pleasure to an indifference to country. For all this there were certain extenuating circumstances. The early Stoic was in close contact with the Cynic and like the later Thoreau, who glorified the life of single blessedness, eschewed the cares of family and preferred solitude to society. Moreover, the first founders of the school, Zeno, Cleanthes, and Chrysippus, being resident foreigners at Athens, could not be citizens and so made a virtue out of a necessity.

Hence arose the Stoic paradoxes—that the good things of life are matters of indifference; that the wise man is absolutely perfect, lord of himself and master of the world; that the sage is a citizen of the world; that local and national ties are not binding, and that even life itself may be thrown off when insult and injury make life intolerable.

The doctrine of things indifferent was a curious compromise. The Stoics declared that only that which is absolutely good, or virtue, can be considered a good; and only that which is absolutely bad, or vice, can be considered an evil. All other things, however great their influence may be on our state, belong to a class of things neither good nor evil, but indifferent. Neither health, nor riches, nor honour, not even life itself, is a good; and just as little are the opposite states—poverty, sickness, disgrace, and death—evils. Such are in themselves indifferent, materials which may be employed either for good or else for evil. Put in another way, some things are to be preferred, others to be avoided, while between the two lies the indeterminate class of things whose value lies in the use made of them. Theoretically the talk of things indifferent implies an attitude of scorn to both the goods and evils of this world, but when utility is brought in there arises a decided compromise with common sense. Consequently not only does a later Stoic like Seneca defend external possessions as aids to virtue, but even Chrysippus allows that it is silly not to desire health, wealth, and freedom from pain.

This admission has been called an anticipation of pragmatism, where the good is defined as the expedient. At any rate, it modifies the doctrine of apathy and runs counter to the second paradox, that the wise man is absolutely perfect. The ordinary Stoic, with his beggar's robe and cropped hair, drew ridicule upon himself when he claimed to be the perfect sage because he was indifferent to the comforts of life. But even the masters were hard put to it to find examples of the perfect sage. Heroes of the mythical Golden Age, like Heracles and Odysseus, hardly fitted the Stoic pattern, while even Socrates was acknowledged to be only a traveller toward virtue.

That the sage was a citizen of the world contained a large measure of truth since theory and practice were congruous. The Stoics were convinced of the solidarity of the race because of the solidarity of the universe. In this great city of the universe, says Epictetus, there is a governor and overseer who orders each and all to fulfil their tasks—the sun to run his course, Agamemnon to lead his army, and all good men to be trained and exercised by God. Now as in Greece all the tribes were called to the Olympian games, so in the greater game of life all contestants enter on an equality and there is no distinction between barbarian and Greek, bond and free.

At this point Epictetus solves these paradoxes in a half-disguised bit of autobiography: "How is it possible that one can live prosperously who hath nothing; a naked, homeless, hearthless, beggarly man, without servants, without a country? Lo, God hath sent you a man to show you in very deed that it is possible. Behold me, that I have neither country, nor house, nor possessions, nor servants; I sleep on the ground; nor is a wife mine, nor children, nor domicile, but only earth and heaven, and a single cloak. And what is lacking to me? do ever I grieve? do I fear? am I not free?"

The lame slave feels himself a citizen of the world, a partaker of universal privileges. His conviction is shared by the aristocratic Seneca, who asserts that birth is of no importance because all are sprung from the gods. So, he argues, the door of virtue is shut to no

ZENO: Founder of Stoicism
DUTY, DEVOTION, SELF-DENIAL

man: it is open to all, admits all, invites all—free men, freedmen, slaves, kings, and exiles. Its election is not of family or fortune; it is content with the bare man.

Such is the system of the Stoics, a doctrine of liberty and equality which is in marked contrast to the teachings of Plato and Aristotle. In the former the most virtuous man is at the top as governor; in the latter the highest virtue consists in solitary contemplation possible only for the man of means. But in this new morality the poor slave could call himself king provided he was ruler of himself. Others have no power over him. When the tyrant says: "I will show you that I am master," the Stoic can reply to him and his guards with their sharp swords: "You may bind the leg and take away the head, but you cannot bind, you cannot take away the will."

This is defiant democracy, based not on conceit but on reason. The Stoic calls himself a servant, but at the same time a sharer in the rule of Zeus. He is thus enabled to draw up this charter of liberty which Epictetus entitles: "How We Should Think as God's Offspring": If those things are true which are said by philosophers concerning the kinship of God and men, what else remains for men to do than after Socrates's way, who never, when men inquired of him what was his native country, replied Athens or Corinth, but the universe. For why wilt thou say thou art an Athenian, and not rather name thyself from that nook alone into which thy wretched body was cast at birth? Is it not plainly from the lordlier place, and that which contains not only that nook and all thy household, but also the whole land whence the race of thy ancestors has come down even to thee, that thou callest thyself Athenian or Corinthian? Whoso, therefore, hath watched the governance of the universe, and hath learned that the greatest and mightiest and amplest of all societies is that which is composed of mankind and of God; and that from Him have descended the seeds not only to my father alone, nor to my grandfather, but to all creatures that are conceived and born upon the earth (but especially to reasoning beings, since to these alone hath nature given it to have communion and intercourse with God, being linked with Him through Reason)—wherefore should such a one not name himself a citizen of the universe? wherefore not a son of God? wherefore shall he fear anything that may come to pass among men? And shall kinship with Cæsar, or with some other of those that are mighty at Rome, be enough to let us live in safety and undespised and fearing nothing at all; but to have God for our maker and father and guardian, shall this not avail to deliver us from griefs and fears?

THE DIFFICULTIES OF THE DOCTRINE

"Some are of opinion that death gives a man courage to support pain, and that pain fortifies a man against death; but I say, rather, that a wise man depends upon himself against both, and that he does not either suffer with patience in hopes of death, or die willingly because he is weary of life, but he bears the one and waits for the other, and carries a divine mind through all the accidents of human life. He looks upon faith and honesty as the most sacred good of mankind, and neither to be forced by necessity nor corrupted by reward. Kill, burn, tear him in pieces, he will be true to his trust; and the more any man labours to make him discover a secret, the deeper he will hide it. Resolution is the inexpugnable defense of human weakness, and it is a wonderful providence that attends it. Horatius Cocles opposed his single body to the whole army, until the bridge was cut down behind him, and then leaped into the river, with his sword in his hand, and came off safe to his party. He is the happy man that is the master of himself, and triumphs over the fear of death, which has overcome the conquerors of the world."
—SENECA, "Of a Happy Life," edited by Walter Clode.

The Stoic is a sharer in the rule of Zeus, a citizen of the universe, but this universe in its lower mundane sphere is by no means one of undiluted happiness. That which stared the Stoic in the face was the misery engendered by military conquests. Even Aristotle with his doctrine of contemplative withdrawal was said to have shown a certain "failure of nerve" when he saw the fall of the independent Greek cities. With the spread of the Macedonian Empire matters grew worse, for the quarrels between Alexander's successors rendered all things insecure; exile, slavery, violent death were possibilities which every man must face. Against these possibilities the philosophers formed a mental security league. The different schools after Aristotle may have been rivals, just as the Greek city-states had been, but they had a common policy against the eventualities of evil. This policy was one of inward peace of mind—in the case of Epicurus through a liberation of man's will from nature's law, in that of Zeno in submission to that law, and in the case of the Eclectics by a utilizing first of one then of another of these doctrines as expediency should demand.

Of these three schools the Stoics were the most successful because the most tough-minded. They alone faced the hardest of practical moral problems, the problem of evil. So against the darts and arrows of outrageous fortune they put on the armour of apathy. Thus they declared that pain was not an evil, because not morally bad, and it was manly to endure it, while they sometimes went so far as to call diseases mere annoyances. However, they were not such foolish illusionists as to deny the existence of evil, as a mere error of mortal mind. Zeno never taught that pain was not painful, while Epictetus compared it to the hardships endured by the athlete: "Thou art about to enter thy name for the Olympic games, O man; no cold and paltry contest. Nor canst thou then be merely overcome and then depart; but first thou must be shamed in the sight of all the world; and not alone of the Athenians, or Lacedemonians, or Nicopolitans. And then if thou hast too rashly entered upon the contest thou must be thrashed, and before being thrashed must suffer thirst and scorching heat, and swallow much dust."

The heat and labour of the day make men tough; hardships are a help to manly virtue. In this way the Stoics sought to explain physical evil, that is, pain and suffering, as a stimulus to fortitude. This is the very spirit of sportsmanship instilled into the Boy Scout and college athlete. "Grin and bear it" is then a Stoic motto illustrated by many an anecdote. Thus Epictetus had his leg broken by his master and simply retorted: "Now you have done it"; while Seneca declared that amid all the extremities of fire and rack men have been found never to groan, never beg for mercy—men who never answered a question, and indeed laughed heartily.

Such instances concern human doings. What of nature's? We may be brave when men use us despitefully, but what shall be our attitude under the vicissitudes of fortune? To this Marcus Aurelius gives an answer: We talk of doctors' orders and say: Æsculapius has prescribed horse exercise, or cold baths, or walking barefoot. It is the same with nature's orders, when she prescribes disease, mutilation, amputation, or some other form of disablement. Just as doctors' orders mean such and such treatment, ordered as specific for such and such state of health, so every individual has circumstances ordered for him specifically in the way of destiny.

This is drifting into the doctrine of necessity. Much pain and suffering, ranging from that of the athlete to that of the ambitious man, come under the caption of "things in our power," and, as such, allow for the play of free will. But there are things not in our power and here free will seems abrogated. Not so, replies the Stoic; our attitude is under our control and if we accept calamities with resignation we are still free. The rational man can thus act because he can see good in apparent evil. If nature prescribes disease and disablement, continues Marcus Aurelius, let us accept such orders as we do the orders of our Æsculapius. They are rough oftentimes, yet we welcome them in hope of health. Try to think of the execution and consummation of nature's good pleasure as you do of bodily good health. Welcome all that comes, perverse though it may seem, for it leads you to the goal, the health of the world order, the welfare and well-being of Zeus. He would not bring this on the individual were it not for the good of the whole.

This is a familiar argument, but it has its flaws. Resignation to calamity is a form of apathy, but while apathy to oneself leads to a rational fortitude, apathy to the sufferings of others leads to emotional callousness. The Stoics are here driven into a corner from which they find it hard to escape; they return to the analogy of the athlete in a curious form. Thus Epictetus gives as an example Socrates before his judges. Socrates, he says, knew how to play ball: and what was the ball that was there thrown about among them? Life, chains, exile, a draught of poison, to be torn from a wife, to leave his children orphans. These were the things among them that they played withal; yet none the less did he play, and flung the ball with proper grace and measure. And so should we do also, having the carefulness of the most zealous players, and yet indifference, as if it were merely about a ball.

This is a poor example and does not present the human spirit of Socrates's apology. He was torn from wife and children, but while the sharp-tongued Xanthippe may not have missed him, his sons did. In other words, the Stoic was often too self-regarding. The general misery might offer him a stage to exhibit his indifference, but that did not obviate the misery of others. The cosmic good must have been cold comfort to orphans.

It was the fault of Stoicism that it made too little of pain. Yet over against this fault must be put the fact that when driven into a narrow pass the Stoic generally exhibited high courage against overwhelming odds. Epictetus's defiance of the tyrant included even the defiance of the great tyrant, Death. In this the Stoics carried to its last issue the double distinction between things to be preferred and avoided and things in our power and not in our power, and sought to solve the problem of man's end by a double paradox. That which most men considered the worst of evils they said should be preferred, and that which men said was not in our power they declared was in our power. By this they meant that arbitrary death at the hands of a tyrant and inevitable death by disease or accident should be scorned, while death by one's own hand should, under certain circumstances, be considered allowable.

In plain language, they justified suicide and called it "reasonable departure from life." The wise man, they said, may take his "free departure" because of a call to sacrifice himself for his country, or because of a tyrant's doing him violence, or because disease hinders the use of the body. But in spite of fair words and an appearance of rationality the Stoics were hard pressed to find cases which justified this dreadful doctrine. They cited the cases of Socrates who drank the hemlock voluntarily and of the younger Cato who fell on his own sword after the defeat at Pharsalia by Cæsar, when the ruin of the commonwealth stared him in the face.

In both these cases the self-immolated victims discoursed on immortality, and were considered models of nobility. But in other cases the Stoics descended to absurdity, as when they cited the case of Zeno, who hanged himself because he had broken his finger, and the case of the aged Cleanthes, who at the command of his physician abstained from food for two days, and then persisted in a course of starvation, saying that it was a pity to retrace his steps as he was now so far upon the road.

The last two cases may be apocryphal, concocted by the enemies of Stoicism. At any rate, they came from a later period of decadence, when suicide became an obsession. However, even in the reign of Nero, a time of violence, cruelty, and lust, Seneca condemned the doctrine of "free departure" as a social disease pointing to morbidity of soul rather than to healthy resolution. Seneca himself was forced to cut his veins because the waiting soldiers saw to it that the orders of the infamous emperor were carried out; but his own view in no way justified the subterfuge of "reasonable departure." He rather took the older Stoic position when he said: "Let every man make the best of life. How terrible is death to one man, which to another appears the greatest providence in nature, even toward all ages and conditions! It is the wish of some, the relief of many, and the end of all. It sets the slave at liberty, carries the banished man home, and places all mortals upon the same level: insomuch that life itself were punishment without it. When I see tyrants, tortures, violences, the prospect of death is a consolation to me, and the only remedy against the injuries of life."

The general attitude of Stoicism is one of courage. Here the models to be imitated are those of the warrior, the athlete, and the gladiator—life is a camp and living soldiers' work; life is a race and the messenger from Marathon will run till he drops dead; life is an arena where men face mortal combat with joy. This is the dominant note, and because of it many a young Stoic, when the new religion from the East came in, was converted to the manly gospel of St. Paul, who had fought the good fight, had run the race, and contended with beasts at Ephesus. In the great apostle they found a Stoic unconscious of his Stoicism, and in the Christian martyr who "met the lion's gory mane," the ideal of Stoic courage.

THE SUPREME PROBLEMS

"For the consciences of the young revolted. Trained at home and in school to believe in providence, in duty, and in patient endurance of evil, they instinctively recognized the Socratic force and example not in the magistrate seated in his curule chair, nor in the rustic priest occupied in his obsolete ritual, but in the teacher on the cross and the martyr on the rack. In ever increasing numbers men, who had from their Stoic education imbibed the principles of the unity of the Deity and the freedom of the will, came over to the new society which professed the one without reservation, and displayed the other without flinching. With them they brought in large measure their philosophic habits of thought, and (in far more particulars than is generally recognized) the definite tenets which the Porch had always inculcated. Stoicism began a new history, which is not yet ended, within the Christian church; and we must now attempt to give some account of this after-growth of the philosophy."—E. VERNON ARNOLD, *Roman Stoicism*.

"Friends," said Epictetus, "wait for God; when he shall give you the signal then go to him." In this advice the Stoic raises the supreme problem of providence, or the moral guidance of the universe, in its relations to the alternative solutions of fate and of fortune. What does philosophy profit you, asks Seneca, if God is the ruler? What, if chance rules? What if all is fated? This last query was based on the solution first offered by the Stoics. Their physics, or philosophy of nature, began with determinism, according to which every event is but a link in an adamantine chain of cause and effect. They start with the apparently meaningless statement that "the universe is." But this is expanded into "Whatever is, is," and the inference drawn is that whatever is cannot be helped. Fate is here contrary to free will and leads to what is called the lazy argument. The classic example is that of sickness. One says to the sick person, "If it is your fate to recover then you will recover whether you call in the physician or not; and if it is your fate not to recover then you will not recover in either case. But it is your fate either to recover or not to recover; therefore it will be useless to call in the physician." This is pure fatalism and the confusion was worse confounded by the answer of Chrysippus that in case of sickness it may be determined by fate that you should both call in a physician and recover.

If, as the early Stoics declared, all these things are equally pre-destined and go together as links in a chain, the universe may be described as a cobweb of causation in which the movement of a single strand affects the entire web. But the talk of chains and cobwebs may be wrong for it makes the universe mechanical and impersonal. According to the majority of Stoics it was not that; it was dynamic and even personal, and as one all-embracing whole included all mental and spiritual characteristics. It started with the fire of Heraclitus, but that fire is at the same time reason, since the nimble flame is not only a symbol of the alert intelligence, but in its steady fixity is itself reason. Hence the primordial fire mist, permeating all things, is both mental and material, and the universe, after the analogy of man who is both mind and body, may be called person.

Such is the Stoic pantheism where nature is identified with God, who is defined as the fashioner of the ordered frame of the universe. This definition disposes of that second alternative offered by Seneca, the alternative of chance. Here the rival school of Epicurus was wont to say that nothing happens by design, but all by chance; that good fortune arises from a lucky throw of nature's dice and bad from an unlucky throw. All events are uncertain because all are due to a fortuitous concourse of atoms; everything occurs at random and nothing according to reason; there is no purpose or fixed end in the universe.

These conclusions are wrong, retorts the Stoic. Chance combinations of atoms explain nothing; there are rhyme and reason in the universe. Atomism would no more account for the designs of provi-dence than alphabets thrown on the ground would account for the composition of the Iliad. Chance is thus disposed of, but another dilemma arises. Are events to be explained as due to blind fate or to seeing providence? The choice makes a great difference and some of the Stoics choose one alternative and others another. Fate, says Zeno, is a power which stirs matter by the same laws and in the same way; it may equally well be called "providence" or "nature." The essence of fate, says Chrysippus, is a spiritual force, duly order-ing the universe; it is the Logos or reason of the universe; it is the law of events providentially ordered in the universe; finally, it is the law by which things that have been, have been; that are, are; that will be, will be.

Thus reason two of the early teachers of the school, but a third, Cleänthes, midway in time between the two, takes a mediating position. This compromiser is for a general providence and in his famous hymn addresses Zeus as "ruler of nature, that governest all things." But the facts of evil remain and Cleänthes cannot hold providence responsible for it. Hence he makes his great exception: "Nor is aught due upon the earth without thee, O God, save the works that evil men do in their folly." To this Stoic leader there is a general providence only in name, for fate is a wider force back of providence, just as in Homer's day it was back of the ruler of Olympus. There was evidently a split in the school, but most of the Stoics followed Chrysippus and believed in a universal, benign providence. To them the universe is a thing of beauty. The heavens are "Time's fair embroidery." Even the terrors of the universe are admirable; storms and lightnings, deluges and earthquakes, call forth awe and wonder. The universe is not only a thing of beauty but a universe of utility. God hath builded thee a great palace, declares Seneca, whose foundations are everlasting, the roof whereof shineth after one sort by day and after another by night . . . and doth not God bestow all benefits upon us? From whence have we so many trees, bearing sundry sorts of savoury fruits; so many wholesome herbs for the maintenance of our healths; such variety of meats answering unto the seasons of the whole year?   .

All this verges toward a belief in a particular providence, yet the Roman statesman warns us that man is apt to swell himself too greatly, as if the world were made for him. As a matter of fact, he points out, only a small part of the world is fit for man to dwell in, while the seasons would roll around even if no man observed them. But other Stoics were not so cautious and the argument sometimes descends from the sublime to the ridiculous. Thus Chrysippus is alleged to have reasoned that horses assist men in fighting, dogs in hunting; lions and leopards provide a discipline in courage; the sow is convenient for sacrifices to the gods, who have given her a soul to serve as salt, and keep the flesh from rotting; the peacock is created for his tail, and the peahen accompanies him for symmetry's sake; the flea is useful to wake us out of sleep, and the mouse to prevent us from being careless in leaving cheese about.

These absurd arguments are attributed to one of the founders of Stoicism, but it may be that such attributions were the work of jealous enemies. However, more dignified difficulties as to the beneficence of nature remain. If all things work together for good, how explain the death of Socrates by poison, the burning alive of Pythagoras, the suicide of Zeno? If the gods care for all men, argues Cicero, it follows logically that they care for each single man. It is but a feeble answer to respond that the gods, who have great things in their charge, must sometimes overlook small matters, just as a good housekeeper is not to be blamed for the loss of some grains of wheat. But what of the wholesale destruction of men and cataclysms such as pestilence and famine, earthquake and conflagration? Here the Stoic at times had recourse to the feeble argument that evil is good in disguise, that pestilence and famine are needed to punish men for their misdeeds, and earthquakes and conflagrations to purify the world from wickedness.

There are echoes of this doctrine of cleansing conflagration in the words of St. Paul, who speaks of the last great day when men shall be purified as by fire, and when the elements shall be melted in a fervent heat. Now Paul the apostle had once been Saul of Tarsus, a city infiltrated with Stoicism. Furthermore, this special doctrine of the moral uses of conflagration has a longer history. It went back to Zeno's authority, Heraclitus, who declares that "fire shall one day come and judge all things." Moreover, to the Stoics God was not only the all-encircling sea of fire called ether, not only the creative rational substance from which the whole universe issues, but a cleansing force which leads to a new creation. In other words, the universe which began as fire shall end as fire. However, this implies construction as well as destruction; there shall be a new heaven and a new earth; the human soul is an emanation from Deity and the warm vital breath shows that it partakes of the supreme soul substance, fire, and is thus penetrated by divinity. Finally, this leads to the assurance that the wise man who has purged his body of the grosser elements shall survive.

Such is the moralized materialism of the Stoics which paradoxically leads to the blessed hope of immortality. And this doctrine of the restitution of all things had still further implications of happiness. As the universe moves in vast cycles, from fire back to fire, so this particular world shall circle back to better times. Though this present age is one of iron, of chain, of dungeon, and of sword, a happier age shall return, the golden age of youth and innocence. The Latin poet Vergil sang of this in his prophecy of the return of the hero when another Jason shall embark in quest of the Golden Fleece, a note reëchoed by the English poet Shelley in his superb lines: "A brighter Hellas rears its mountains from waves serener far."

The Stoic doctrine of the restitution of all things is bound up with the theory of recurrent cycles in which history repeats itself and what once was shall be again. Plato had once derided this doctrine when he put into the mouth of a certain Pythagorean this statement: "I with this little rod in my hands shall some day once again be addressing you, my class, sitting around me precisely as you sit now, and everything else in like manner will recur precisely as before."

This quaint notion was concocted by the Pythagoreans to uphold their doctrine of the transmigration of souls. A similar speculation is also in use among the Epicureans who with their infinite number of atoms, infinite time, and infinite space argue as did their poet Lucretius that the same combination of circumstances can recur again and again. But with these views the Stoics would have nothing to do; they came from rival schools as did the doctrine of the Aristotelians, who held that the existing order of things is fixed forever as it is. No, the doctrines of the great conflagration and of the eternal return go back to Heraclitus, the philosopher of fire and flux and of the guiding reason. The Stoic founder caught his spirit and his followers moralized it. Whatever, then, befall us, whatever the vicissitudes of fortune, we shall trust in providence, play our part, and quit ourselves like men.

II. EPICUREANISM

". . . For Epicurus the purpose of retirement was primarily the desire to escape so far as possible the incursions of society, with no thought of fitting himself for citizenship in another world. To this end political life was to be utterly eschewed; for how, indeed, could the philosopher maintain his precious calm of soul, while suffering the anxieties of ambition or the envies of office? To the same end marriage and the cares of a family were to be avoided, though not so rigorously as political entanglements. In one respect Epicurus was better than his creed. It is notorious that his school made much of friendship, theoretically and practically; and their kindly comradeship, even their readiness to sacrifice ease and possessions for a friend, threw something like a glow of romance over their otherwise unlovely profession of egotism. No doubt Epicurus could find logical excuses for this human weakness in the mutual protection offered by such unions, but in fact some inextinguishable nobility of mind carried him here quite beyond the bounds of his boasted principles. His hedonism might leave a place open for friendship as the greatest felicity which wisdom procures for the whole of life, but he was surely forgetting the claims of the flesh when he added that it was of more account to know with whom we were to eat and drink than what we were to eat and drink. And his rejection of the Pythagorean community of goods (which had been so alluring to Plato), because it shows some lack of confidence in the generosity of friendship, is one of the finest and, in the French sense of the word, most *spirituel* of ancient maxims.

"Such was the social ideal of Epicurus, and his rules for private conduct were of a piece with it—they were directed as completely, considering the place of friendship in his social scheme even more completely, toward the attainment of that outer and inner security on which the continuous state of pleasure must depend. To this end morality of a sort is necessary: 'It is not possible to live pleasantly without living wisely and fairly and justly, nor to live wisely and fairly and justly without living pleasantly.'"—PAUL ELMER MORE, *Hellenistic Philosophies.*

THE SCHOOL OF DELIVERANCE

In contrast to Stoicism with its doctrine of duty comes Epicureanism with its doctrine of pleasure. Both sought to discover the chief end of life; the Stoic drew up a scheme which in the main is plain and practical; the Epicurean is more subtle. To achieve a perfect equilibrium between pleasure and pain, so that a state of undisturbedness shall result, is more difficult than to count pleasure as but dust in the balance. To the Stoic the good things of life could be disregarded as of no account; to his rival the pleasurable quality was the thing to be considered. By a strange paradox the simple things might give the finest sensation—if hunger is the best sauce, bread and water is a feast.

The goal of both movements was the simple life, but the roads by which they sought their goal were different; the one being that of renunciation, the other that of calculation. The Stoic made it his rule "to do without," and let life go at that; his rival considered what he should do without and for what reason. His was a studied effort so to pick and choose that he might achieve the pleasantest sensation. The limit of pleasure, says Epicurus, is obtained by calculating the pleasures themselves and the contrary pains.

The Epicureans' method of calculation is in marked contrast to that of the Stoics. The latter sought to solve the problem of life by erasing pleasures; the former by pondering over their uses. If you reject absolutely any single sensation without stopping to discriminate, they explained, you will throw into confusion even the rest of your sensations by your groundless belief, so as to reject the truth altogether. Truth, then, lies in considering all factors, and the search for the right sensation resembles the construction of one of those magic squares where the final identical sums are obtained only after the most careful placing of the digits. There is a certain fascination in the Epicurean scheme because of its very subtlety. Whatever way you look at it the results are consistent. It works not only positively but negatively. If life is the summation of sensations, death is their subtraction. Hence arises the paradox of the privative, as when Epicurus boldly asserts: "Death is nothing to us; for the body, when it has been resolved into its elements, has no feeling, and that which has no feeling is nothing to us."

This is one of the "golden" maxims of the founder of the school of pleasure and offers a challenge to the founder of the school of duty, for where Zeno made death a call to courage, Epicurus made it a matter of no account. All this moral arithmetic sounds cold-blooded, but it serves to correct the popular conception that the Epicurean doctrine was one of fleshly indulgence. Calculation is mental, and as a criterion to pleasure served to show that mere animal pleasures are not to be desired. Consider the voluptuary. Epicurus does not censure him but only analyzes him: If the objects which are productive of pleasure to profligate persons really free them from fears of the mind—the fear of death, the fear of pain—we should not have any reason to censure such persons. But do the latter consider these consequences? No, says Epicurus, the flesh assumes the limits of pleasure to be infinite, and only infinite time would satisfy it. But the mind, grasping in thought what the end and limit of the flesh is, and banishing the terrors of futurity, procures a complete and perfect life and has no longer any need of infinite time. However, continues this mathematical moralist, let us not accuse the flesh as the cause of great evil, neither let us attribute our distresses to outward things. Let us rather seek the causes of this distress within our own souls, and let us cut off every vain craving and hope for things which are fleeting, and let us become only masters of ourselves.

The musings of Epicurus take the form of an inner dialogue between the mind and the flesh and exhibit a spirit of detachment which is the strength of his system. In fact, his cool and calculating attitude caused a certain feverish irritation in his rivals. The man

who addresses his warring members as if they were litigants in a law-
suit is a judge, and judges are formidable opponents. The jury may
be moved by sentimental appeals; not so Epicurus. Thus he pro-
pounds this case: Public speaking abounds in heart throbs and in
anxiety whether you can carry conviction. Why, then, pursue an
object like this, which is at the disposal of others?

With all his talk about feelings Epicurus is no vapid sentimental-
ist. He is a calculating rationalist who scrutinizes the false beliefs
of his fellow-men. One of his aims, therefore, is to free poor humanity
of its delusions. Legend has it that as a boy he used to accompany
his mother when she went about the small cottages, performing the
purifications, and that he used to read the magic formula. However,
when he grew up he strove to remove such vulgar superstitions.
Men, he declared, "live in dread of what the legends tell us, fears,
I mean, inspired by celestial and atmospheric phenomena, the fear
of death, the fear of pain. . . . There would be no advantage in providing security against our fellow-men so long as we were alarmed
by occurrences over our heads or beneath the earth, or in general
by whatever happens in the infinite void."

In these strictures Epicurus had an end in view which he achieved
with such success that the poet Menander sings his fame as one who
"freed his country from foolishness." But the legends he attacked
were not so much the old discredited mythology as the new superstitions filtering in from the East. The chief of these was astrology.
The great Persian king had long since been defeated, but there now
arose a Persian or Chaldean worship of the gods—"bright poten-
tates, shining in the fire of heaven." Aristotle's successor, Theophrastus, was reported to have said that the most extraordinary
thing of his age was the lore of the Chaldeans, who foretold not only
events of public interest but even the lives and deaths of individuals.

These wise men of the East did not seem so wise to Epicurus.
No stars in their courses ever fought for him, nor did comets and
eclipses trouble his tranquillity. Besides the fears inspired by
celestial and atmospheric phenomena he mentions the fear of death
and the fear of pain. He asserts that these may be obviated. Death he
has already said "is nothing to us," and pain, he adds, even if extreme, is present a very short time. For these reasons, he argues,
men should drop their apprehensions; fears are foolish and a foolish
life is restless and disagreeable; it is wholly engrossed with the future.

Properly interpreted, these are significant statements. Fears, in
the original Greek, were phobias, and the cure of phobias suggests
the modern psychiatrist or physician of the soul. In other words,

Epicurus was not so much the founder of a philosophy of pleasure as the founder of a school of mental hygiene. So the constant use of the phrase "the health of the soul" makes Epicurus an early advocate of mental medicine. The ancient conditions were of course in many ways different from the modern. Astrology and mythology are obsolete, but there remain countless worries over religious problems and over the hazards of life and over business and public affairs. All these psychic tensions are mentioned by Epicurus and also means for their relief. There is the baffling problem of religious pathology from the fear of dying to the fear of committing the unpardonable sin. Fragments of the teachings of Epicurus suggest his treatment of the anxious soul: "Learn betimes to die, or if you like it better, to pass over to the gods. . . . The knowledge of sin is the beginning of salvation." These religious anxieties, he continues, are based on certain fundamental phobias which must first be removed. Here the study of nature shows that the fear of death, the fear of the gods, the fear of divine retribution are all alike chimerical; they are false apprehensions based on ignorance. The utterances of the multitude about the gods are not true preconceptions but false assumptions. . . . Verily there are gods, but they are not such as the multitude believe.

This is negative advice and tends to remove fear; positive advice follows and fear is supplanted by hope and that in turn by a most modern device, "the will to believe." "Those things which without ceasing I have declared unto thee, those do and exercise thyself therein, holding them to be the elements of right life. First, believe that God is a being blessed and immortal, according to the notion of a God commonly held amongst men; and so believing, thou shalt not affirm of him aught that is contrary to immortality or that agrees not with blessedness, but shalt believe about him whatsoever may uphold both his blessedness and his immortality."

Suppressed complexes due to religion are thus treated by a thinker falsely charged with atheism. But there are more subtle problems remaining. These concern not the fear of death but the fear of life itself. Here Epicurus first excludes that class of men who argue in laboured fashion that life is not worth living and that all is vanity; these are the professional pessimists who extract a certain amount of pleasure from constructing their sombre systems. They are really tough-minded. But there is a larger class of ordinary people, the tender-minded, "the sick souls," who are afraid of living itself and suffer from constant anxieties and apprehensions over their daily tasks. They are afflicted in varying degrees with the inferiority complex; they are the social snails who draw into their shells, the timid souls who were born bashful and prefer solitude to society. Virtually Epicurus says to these: "Come into my garden, memorize my maxims, repeat them daily, and your worries will disappear." Actually he defines philosophy as "a daily business of speech and thought to secure a happy life." Thus he begins his letter to his disciple Menœceus: "Let no one be slow to seek wisdom when he is young nor weary in the search thereof when he is grown old. For no age is too early or too late for the health of the soul. And to say that the season for philosophy has not yet come, or that it is passed and gone, is like saying that the season for happiness is not yet or that it is now no more. Therefore, both old and young ought to seek wisdom, that so a man as age comes over him may be young in good things, because of the grace of what has been, and while he is young may likewise be old, because he has no fear of the things which are to come. So we must exercise ourselves in the things which bring happiness, since, if that be present, we have everything and, if that be absent, all our actions are directed toward attaining it."

This letter is extraordinarily modern in spirit and so is a later inscription which was but recently discovered. A certain Diogenes of Cappadocia, an Epicurean teacher in an obscure town of Asia Minor in the century of Marcus Aurelius, wished to leave the teachings of Epicurus in a permanent form and caused an inscription to be made. This runs in part as follows: "This writing shall speak for me as if I were present, striving to prove that nature's good, namely tranquillity of mind, is the same for one and all. . . . Since the vast majority of men suffer from the plague of false opinions the number of victims increases—for in mutual emulation they catch the contagion one from another like sheep—I wish to make use of this portico to exhibit in a public place the remedy which brings salvation. For thus I banish the vain terrors which hold us in subjection, eradicating some pains altogether and confining such as are due to nature within very moderate bounds and reducing them to the smallest dimensions."

The system of Epicurus which his enemies denounced as atheistic and immoral turns out to be an ancient combination of religion and mental medicine. Calumny represents the Master's garden in Athens as a place of luxury and gilded vice, but the inscription placed at the entrance of the garden does not bear this out. It runs as follows: "The hospitable keeper of this mansion, where you will find pleasure the highest good, will present you liberally with barley cakes and water fresh from the spring. The gardens will not provoke your appetite by artificial dainties, but satisfy it with natural supplies. Will you not be well entertained?"

What Epicurus really taught was the art of life for those who found life difficult, first by removing false notions gained in youth and then, if needs be, by withdrawing from society according to the maxim "Live concealed." The efficacy of the system lies in the first of these measures, but only in the second if it be taken figuratively. Few of his followers could live with the Master in his garden, yet all of his successors could erect a mental wall against the outside world. Here they had his own advice: Do everything as if Epicurus had his eye upon you. Retire into yourself chiefly at that time when you are compelled to be in a crowd.

MENTAL HYGIENE

Epicurus has been criticized for advocating a flight from society. He assuredly makes too broad a generalization when he declares that man is not by nature adapted for living in civic communities and in civilization. However, there remains the not inconsiderable class of people who find life difficult. For these the simple life is the thing and it is for these that Epicurus added the maxim: "The wise man will be fond of living in the country." This is also a counsel of perfection, hence for the city dweller some substitute must be offered. This substitute is mental freedom and its corollaries. The whole matter is summed up in this remarkable saying: The most precious fruit of independence and plain living is freedom.

There are many implications in this advice. Plain living is obvious; the twin brother of the strong mind is the strong body; no cure of mental trouble, great or small, can be effected without a careful regimen. The need for health is obvious; that for independence is more subtle for it offers a real defense mechanism against the mental complex. Or as Epicurus puts it in a better way: Let us become wholly masters of ourselves by seeking the causes of distress within our souls.

To cultivate the feeling of independence is the first advice of this physician of souls. It is in very childhood, he explains, that we have gained those fears engendered by false notions of the universe. Old Homer was a fabricator of myths, but much worse is he who says that it were good not to be born, but when once one is born to pass with all haste through the gates of Hades. Who this false adviser, who this pessimist was Epicurus does not say, but he asks sarcastically: If he in truth believes this, why does he not depart from life?

EPICURUS
A Misunderstood Philosopher

This reference may be to the Cynics; more obvious are the references to the Stoics, who so often confused providence, chance, and fortune. To them the Epicurean makes this reply: Destiny, which some introduce as sovereign over all things, the wise man laughs to scorn, affirming that certain things happen of necessity, others by chance, others through our own agency. For he sees that necessity destroys responsibility and that chance or fortune is inconstant; whereas our own actions are free. This call to intellectual freedom is a dominant note in the teachings of Epicurus and he concludes his letter to Menœceus with these words: "Exercise thyself in these and kindred precepts day and night, both by thyself and with him who is like unto thee; then never, either in waking or in dream, wilt thou be disturbed but wilt live as a god amongst men."

It is surprising to see how closely the Epicurean rules for the health of the soul fit into the most recent schemes of mental hygiene. It is for this reason that we may interpret his call to mental independence as a defense mechanism against an inferiority complex. The Stoics implied as much, without the use of the modern scientific jargon, when they charged the "Garden Philosophers" with being weak and effeminate, unable to face the hazards of life. The charge is partly true. Epicurus advised his followers to live the hidden life, to avoid society and civic duties, "unless something extraordinary should occur." This timidity and aloofness may be explained by the poor health of the founder. As a boy, according to one account, he had to be lifted down from his chair and had so sensitive a skin that he could not bear any clothing heavier than a tunic. Another account states that he was in so pitiable a state of health that he could not for many years arise from his couch. Further and fully authentic details have come down to us in a final letter to his disciple Idomeneus: "On this last, yet blessed, day of my life, I write to you. Pains and tortures of body I have to the full, but there is set over against these the joy of my heart at the memory of our happy conversations in the past."

Adding to his invalidism the fact that Epicurus lived when very difficult times oppressed Greece, we have an explanation of his advice to his followers to live the hidden life and to avoid society and public affairs. This advice substantiates the charge of the Stoics that the Epicureans neglected civic duties, yet what the latter lacked in practical activity they made up in intellectual agility. The type is familiar. The Epicureans were social egotists, ancient representatives of that modern intelligentsia who exercise their brains in criticizing the structure of society. They may be afraid of much, but they are not afraid of expressing their opinions. They are not utter pessimists, for they take an unholy pleasure in hitting the heads of the conventional. They may be called pacifists who are afraid of the firing line, but they are certainly not afraid of the consequences of their criticism.

This is the modern type, familiar in the Great War. The ancient type was not unlike it. We have at least two records of Epicureans being banished by the authorities, and banishment in those days was no light thing. To say the least, the Epicureans, with all their words about not meddling with other people's affairs in order to avoid pain, did a good deal of meddling. They attacked the current conventions not only in religion but in politics, and criticism of the latter in classic days brought severer penalties than the former. There was as yet no Holy Roman Empire, but the state itself was counted holy. For criticizing it the entire body of philosophers— Epicureans, Stoics, and Eclectics—were at one time banished from Rome by the emperor Domitian. Here we may well expect that the Epicureans were the chief trouble makers, for when the Stoics advised participation in the activities of the state the Epicureans cast doubts upon the very foundations of the state itself.

Thus the Stoic charge of their opponents' timidity falls flat when applied to the intellectual sphere. Epicurus showed himself a radical in political science when he made these bold statements as to jurisprudence. There never was an absolute justice, runs one of the golden sentences, but only a convention made in mutual intercourse, in whatever region, from time to time, providing against the infliction or suffering of harm.

The conservative upholder of eternal justice would consider this a highly subversive sentiment, but more of the same kind is to follow: Natural justice is a contract of expediency. . . . Whatever in conventional law is attested to be expedient in the needs arising out of mutual intercourse, this law is by its nature just. . . . But where the conventional laws, when judged by their consequences, were seen not to correspond with the notion of justice, such laws were not really just.

Put in more recent language, this is radically pragmatic. The law as such is to be considered artificial, conventional, and expedient, "so long as we do not trouble ourselves about empty terms, but look broadly at the facts." For these statements Epicurus has been called practical, realistic, and modern, a radical whose views ran counter to the pagan notion of the omnipotent state. As such he was the anticipator in political science of Hobbes in his doctrine of natural law as mutual agreement, of Hume in his government based on the common consent of mankind, and of Rousseau in his social contract. Epicurus was bold in theory but not in practice. The Epicureans, declares Plutarch, shun politics as the ruin and confusion of true happiness. Now happiness is the sum of tranquillity, and tranquillity Epicurus pronounced to be "the alpha and omega of a perfect life." From this definition, then, there logically follows this advice of the master: When safety on the side of man has been tolerably secured, it is by quiet and by withdrawing from the multitude that the most complete tranquillity is to be found.

This is a fatal admission of surrender, yet it is characteristic of that type of verbal reformers who are not real reformers—armchair critics who while denouncing the law take advantage of the law whenever their rights of personal liberty and free speech are threatened. The Epicureans have been excused for not engaging in rough-and-tumble politics because such avoidance is the common practice of mankind in a period of despotism. It is true that the Greek provinces under Roman rule were no Elysian fields of freedom, but we know of no case where any Epicurean followed even this exceptional case mentioned by the Master: A wise man will not enter upon political life unless something extraordinary should occur.

With such advice we may speculate as to the number of followers of Epicurus. The system rightly understood was so subtle that it probably had but few genuine adherents. The Stoics could cite among their number those who, like Epictetus the slave, taught civic duty and others, like Seneca the statesman and Marcus Aurelius the emperor, who carried on in all the cares and perplexities of state. But Epicurus had no such following. The most famous exponent of his doctrine was the Roman Lucretius, who in his speculative poem, *On the Nature of Things,* gave an extraordinary picture of the rise of mankind from savagery to civilization and took as his dominant motive the freeing of the mind from superstitious fears. In portraying "man's life upon earth in base dismay," he exclaims, "So great are the evils wrought by religion." Besides a radical attack on conventional statecraft, the freeing of man from the religious complex appears to be a fundamental aim of Epicurus. The whole matter is summed up with incisive brevity in the portico inscription of the ancient Diogenes of Cappadocia: Nothing to fear in God: Nothing to feel in death: Good can be attained: Evil can be endured.

So much for the last of the pagan schools. In contrast to this doctrine of surrender we turn to the Christian philosopher St.

Augustine, whose great work, *On the City of God*, may be summarized in this fourfold opposite statement: Everything to hope in God: Everything to feel after death: Good cannot be attained in this life: Evil cannot be endured—except for the grace of God and the blessed hope of immortality.

Breinigsville, PA USA
17 December 2010
251657BV00003B/39/P